W9-CBC-774

Stegosaurus

by Wil Mara

Content Consultant

Gregory M. Erickson, PhD
Paleontologist
The Florida State University
Tallahassee, Florida

Reading Consultant

Jeanne Clidas
Reading Specialist

Children's Press®
An Imprint of Scholastic Inc.
New York Toronto London Auckland Sydney
Mexico City New Delhi Hong Kong
Danbury, Connecticut

Library of Congress Cataloging-in-Publication Data

Mara, Wil.

Stegosaurus/by Wil Mara.

p. cm.—(Rookie read-about dinosaurs)

Includes bibliographical references and index.

ISBN-13: 978-0-531-20860-1 (lib. bdg.)   ISBN-10: 0-531-20860-5 (lib. bdg.)

ISBN-13: 978-0-531-20929-5 (pbk)   ISBN-10: 0-531-20929-6 (pbk)

1. Stegosaurus—Juvenile literature. I. Title. II. Series.

QE862.O65M246 2012

567.9153—dc23   2011031703

Printed in China 62

SCHOLASTIC, CHILDREN'S PRESS, ROOKIE READ-ABOUT®, and associated logos are trademarks and/or registered trademarks of Scholastic Inc.

1 2 3 4 5 6 7 8 9 10 R 21 20 19 18 17 16 15 14 13 12

Photographs © 2012: Black Hills Institute of Geological Research, Inc./
Timothy Larson: 28, 29; Bridgeman Art Library/Look and Learn: cover, 10, 11;
DK Images: 16, 17 (Andy Crawford), 14, 31 top left; Getty Images/De Agostini
Picture Library: 6, 7, 31 top right, 31 bottom right; iStockphoto/Allan Tooley: 8,
9, 31 bottom left; National Geographic Stock/Charles R. Knight: 22, 31
bottom left; Photo Researchers: 26 (Ludek Pesek), 24, 25 (Mark Hallett
Paleoart), 4 (Richard Bizley); Superstock, Inc./De Agostini: 18, 20.

TABLE OF CONTENTS

MEET THE STEGOSAURUS

The Stegosaurus (steg-uh-SAWR-uss) was a dinosaur. It ate plants. It did not eat other animals.

It had bony plates on its back.

The Stegosaurus
had long back legs.
It had short front legs.

The Stegosaurus had
a very small brain.
Its brain was about
the size of a walnut.

HOW BIG?

The Stegosaurus was almost as long as a school bus! The Stegosaurus was as heavy as an elephant!

EATING RIGHT

The Stegosaurus had a beak. It used its beak to pick up plants.

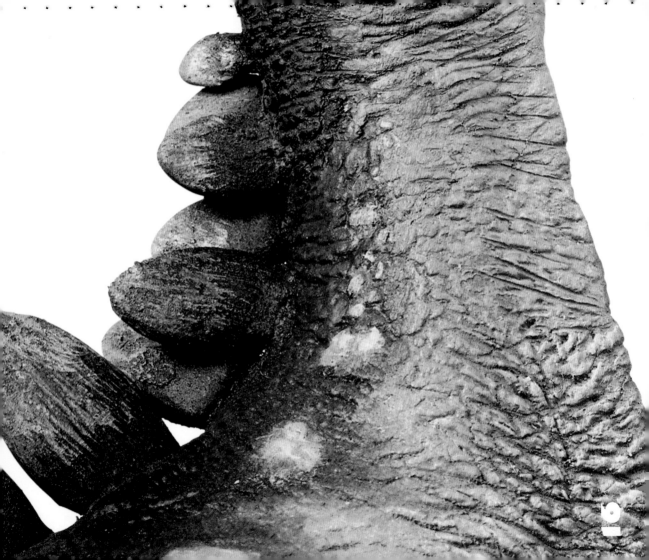

It had teeth in its cheeks.
The teeth were small and flat.

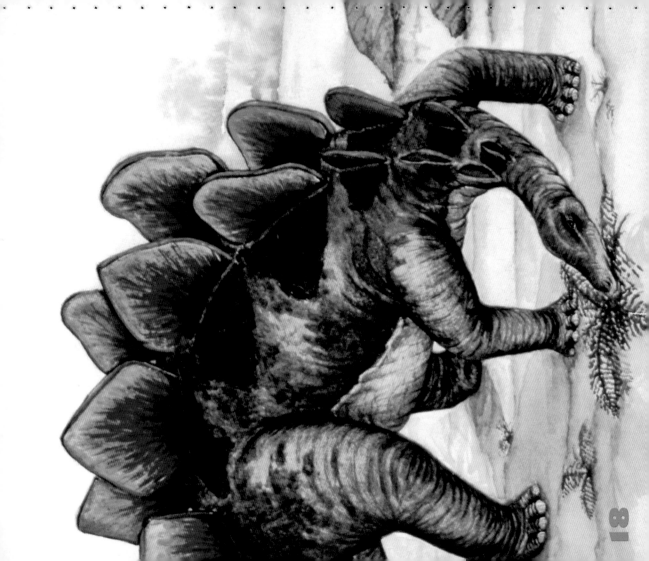

It used its flat teeth to chew leaves and small branches.

The Stegosaurus might have stood up on its back legs. Then it could reach fruit in tall trees.

STAY AWAY, ENEMIES!

The Stegosaurus was big and slow. It did not run from enemies.

But it had spikes on its tail.

It used the spikes to fight.

The plates on the back made
it hard for another dinosaur
to bite a Stegosaurus.

DINOSAUR BONES

Scientists found
Stegosaurus bones.
They built a skeleton from
the bones. It is in a museum.

Can you find the bony plates
on the back of the skeleton?

Can you find the spikes
on the skeleton tail?

TRY THIS! Ask your child if she can recall from the book how the Stegosaurus used its spikes (to fight enemies). Go back in the book with your child to find the bony plates and tail spikes in the illustration on pages 10-11. Comparing the skeleton with the illustrations is a fun way to talk with your child about what he just read.

STEGOSAURUS FACT FILE

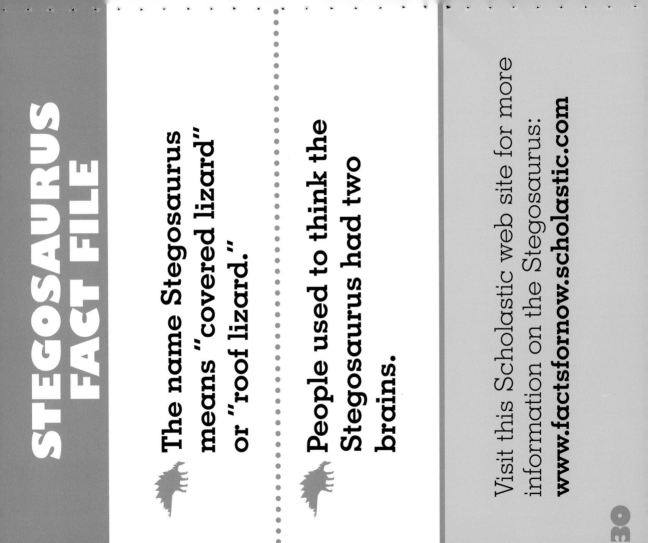

The name Stegosaurus means "covered lizard" or "roof lizard."

People used to think the Stegosaurus had two brains.

Visit this Scholastic web site for more information on the Stegosaurus: **www.factsfornow.scholastic.com**

leaves

Stegosaurus

plate

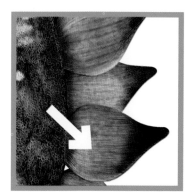

spike

Index

Learn More!

You can learn more about the Stegosaurus at:

www.amnh.org/exhibitions/dinosaurs/display/colorful.php

About the Author

Wil Mara is the award-winning author of more than 100 books, many of them educational titles for young readers. More information about his work can be found at www.wilmara.com.